LIGHTNING
BOLT
BOOKS™

How Do Tanks Work?

Buffy Silverman

Lerner Publications ◆ Minneapolis

Lerner Publications Company
A division of Lerner Publishing Group, Inc.
241 First Avenue North
Minneapolis, MN 55401 USA

For reading levels and more information, look up this title at www.lernerbooks.com.

Library of Congress Cataloging-in-Publication Data

Silverman, Buffy, author.
　　How do tanks work? / Buffy Silverman.
　　pages cm — (Lightning bolt books. How vehicles work)
　　Summary: "Young readers will love this exciting, in-depth yet accessible look at tanks,
including how they work, the special equipment they need, and what makes them the toughest
all-terrain vehicles on the planet"—Provided by publisher.
　　Audience: 5–8.
　　Audience: K–3.
　　Includes bibliographical references and index.
　　ISBN 978-1-4677-9502-9 (lb : alk. paper) — ISBN 978-1-4677-9685-9 (pb : alk. paper) —
ISBN 978-1-4677-9686-6 (eb pdf)
　　1. Tanks (Military science)—Juvenile literature. I. Title.
UG446.5.S5535　2015
623.74'752—dc23　　　　　　　　　　　　　　　　　　　　　2015017444

Manufactured in the United States of America
1 – BP – 12/31/15

Table of Contents

On the Move

A tank speeds over desert sand. It plows through mud. It climbs hills and crashes through fences.

A tank's tracks are steel links that are joined together. They help a tank travel over rough land. They grip the ground.

This tank's tracks are built to be tough!

Tanks are heavy. The tracks spread the tank's weight over a large area. The tank does not sink into the ground.

The tank's wheels are inside the tracks. Two wheels have spikes. The spiked wheels turn the tracks. These wheels are called sprockets.

This is a sprocket.

Powerful Engines

The main part of a tank is the hull. The engine is in the rear of the hull.

The engine turns fuel into power that makes a tank move. A tank's engine works like a jet engine.

Air is sucked into the engine. The air is pressed in a small space. Fuel is added to the air. The fuel and the air burn. They spin a turbine.

A turbine is like a fan. Hot gases make turbines spin.

These tracks stir up dust as they move.

A rod connects the turbine to the sprockets. The spinning turbine turns the sprockets. The tracks move.

Heavy tanks burn a lot of fuel.
They must carry a lot of fuel.

This soldier fuels a tank.

There are 500 gallons (1,893 liters) of fuel in this tank. That's enough liquid to fill your bathtub eleven times!

Giant Guns

The top of a tank is the turret. The turret sits on the hull. Guns are on the turret.

Soldiers can aim a tank's guns by turning a gear on the hull.

A gear on the hull connects to a gear inside the turret. A gear is a wheel with teeth. The teeth on two gears fit into one another. When the gear on the hull turns, the turret spins.

The crew turns the turret to aim the large cannon. The turret can turn in a complete circle. Smaller guns on top of the tank also turn.

A cannon is a huge gun that is too heavy for a person to carry.

Sensors are on the outside of a tank. They measure a tank's position and wind speed.

This is a sensor. Sensors can measure wind speed and many other things.

A computer in the tank gets information from sensors. The computer helps aim the guns.

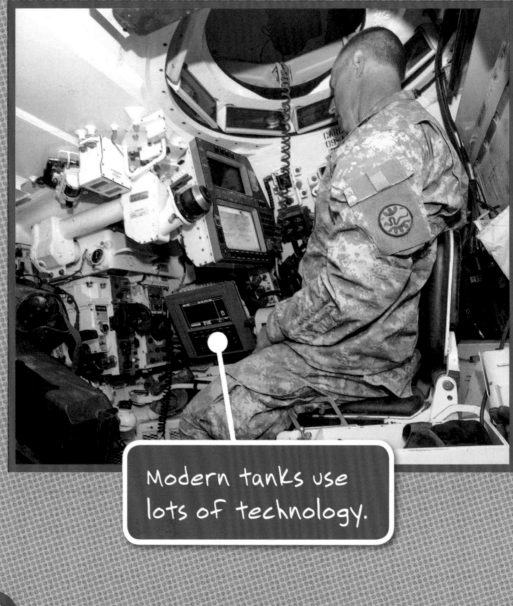

Modern tanks use lots of technology.

A tank crew can aim in the dark. A sensor measures heat coming from objects. It makes a picture for the crew based on the heat.

Tough Armor

Heavy armor covers a tank. The armor is two layers of steel plates. Between the steel are tiles and open space.

Armor protects this soldier when he's inside his tank.

Bullets and missiles may pierce the outer layer of steel. But they do not reach the crew. The bullets and missiles are trapped in the tiles.

Bullets cannot break through this tough tank.

The crew launches smoke grenades. The tank disappears in a cloud of smoke.

Smoke grenades help keep a tank from being seen.

Filters clean the air that the crew breathes. The filters keep the crew safe from harmful chemicals.

The air inside a tank is clean and safe for soldiers to breathe.

Meet the Crew

Four people work inside each tank. The driver sits in the front of the hull. Sensors and cameras let him see outside. He steers the tank and controls its speed.

Other members of the crew ride in the turret. The commander is in charge. He views the battlefield and makes a plan.

This commander makes a plan for his crew.

The loader loads the cannon with ammunition. The gunner fires the cannon. A laser on the tank measures the distance to the target.

Ammunition is shot from weapons. Ammunition includes bullets for guns and shells for cannons.

Tanks are the toughest vehicles on land. They're ready to roll anywhere in the world!

Diagram

turret

hull

tracks

cannon

wheels

sprocket

Tank

Fun Facts

- Troops first used tanks in battle during World War I (1914–1918).

- An M1 Abrams tank can reach speeds of 45 miles (72 kilometers) per hour. It weighs from 60 to 70 tons (54 to 64 metric tons).

- The tanks of the future will probably be smaller and lighter. The US Army is planning a new tank that can drop to the ground from an airplane.

Glossary

armor: a hard covering that protects something

engine: a machine that gives a tank energy to move

gear: a wheel with teeth

hull: the main body of a tank

sensor: a piece of equipment that responds to motion, light, or temperature

smoke grenade: a small bomb that makes smoke

sprocket: a wheel with spikes that turns the tracks of a tank

turbine: a part of an engine that has blades that spin

turret: the top part of a tank that turns and includes the main cannon

Further Reading

American Heroes Channel: Greatest Tank Battles
http://www.ahctv.com/weapons-technology/videos/tank-battles

LaPadula, Tom. *Learn to Draw Tanks, Aircraft & Armored Vehicles.* Irvine, CA: Walter Foster, 2011.

Nagelhout, Ryan. *Tanks.* New York: Gareth Stevens, 2015.

National Army Museum Tank Game
http://www.armymuseum.co.nz/education/kids-zone/games

National Museum, United States Army: Rhino Tank
http://thenmusa.org/rhino-tank-1.php

Silverman, Buffy. *How Do Jets Work?* Minneapolis: Lerner Publications, 2013.

Index

Photo Acknowledgments

The images in this book are used with the permission of: US Army/HQ VCorps/VCI/ Richard Bumgardner, p. 2; © Ed Darack/SuperStock, p. 4; © RGB Ventures/SuperStock/ Alamy, p. 5; US Army photo by Staff Sgt. John Couffe, p. 6; US Army photo by Sgt. Ian Schell, p. 7; US Army photo by Sgt. Ken Scar, p. 8; Lance Cpl. Paul Torres/US Marines, p. 9; © Nabonaco/flickr.com, p. 10; Spc. Chase Kincaid/United States Department of Defense, p. 11; Gunnery Sgt. Chad R. Kiehl/US Marines, p. 12; Staff Sgt. Brian Lautenslager/US Marines, p. 13; Sgt. Devin Nichols/US Marines, p. 14; US Army photo by Sgt. Brandon Banzhaf, p. 15; US Army photo by Lt. Austin McGuin, p. 16; US Army photo by Sgt. Quentin Johnson, p. 17; US Army photo by Maj. Wayne (Chris) Clyne, p. 18; US Army photo by Staff Sgt. Grady Jones, p. 19; Cpl. Marco Mancha/US Marines, p. 20; MSGT Howard J. Farrell/US Marines, p. 21; © Staff Sgt. Anthony Housey/Minnesota Army National Guard/flickr.com (CC BY-ND 2.0), p. 22; US Army photo by 1st. Lt. Joseph Brown, p. 23; Sgt. Sara Wood/United States Department of Defense, p. 24; Staff Sgt. Suzanne M. Day/United States Department of Defense, p. 25; Cpl. Timothy Childers/US Marines, p. 26; Cpl. Chelsea Flowers/US Marines, p. 27; © Laura Westlund/Independent Picture Service, p. 28; Sgt. John Raufmann/US Marines, p. 31.

Front cover: US Army Photo by 7th Army Joint Multinational Training Command (CC BY 2.0.

Main body text set in Johann Light 30/36.